D0020418

IN THEIR OW

POCAHONTAS

George Sullivan

SCHOLASTIC
REFERENCE

LIBRARY OF CONGRESS CATALOGING-IN-PUBLICATION DATA

Sullivan, George, 1927–
Pocahontas/George Sullivan
p.   cm.—(In their own words)
Includes bibliographical references and index.
1. Pocahontas, d. 1617—Juvenile literature.   2. Powhatan Indians—Biography—Juvenile literatuture.   3. Jamestown (Va.)—History—Juvenile literature.
4. Powhatan Indians—History—Juvenile literature.   [1. Pocahontas, –d. 1617.
2. Powhatan Indians—Biography.   3. Indians of North America—Virginia—Biography.   4. Women—Biography.   5. Smith, John, 1580–1631.   6. Jamestown (Va.)—History.]   I. Title.   II. In their own words (Scholastic)
E99.P85 P5795   2001
975.5′01′092—dc21
[B]   00-057382
ISBN 0-439-32668-0 (pob)
ISBN 0-439-16585-7 (pb)

10 9 8 7 6 5 4   02 03 04 05 06

Composition by Brad Walrod
Printed in the U.S.A.   23

First trade printing, March 2002

CONTENTS

INTRODUCTION

S HE WAS PROBABLY ROUND-FACED, with "thick black hair, shaven close." She was of "a Coulour [color] browne."

She had "handsome lymbes [limbs] and slender armes [arms]." These and her face may have been heavily tattooed.

She probably wore a headband, decorated beads, and earrings. Her head and shoulders may have been coated with red powder. This had been "mixed with the oyle [oil] of the walnut or Beares [bear's] grease."

She was unusual for her "wit and spirit."

Her name was Matoaka. But she was nicknamed Pocahontas. It meant "playful, sportive, frisky."

These descriptive words and phrases are from books written about 400 years ago.

The story of Pocahontas is well known. She was the "dearest daughter" of the Native American chief Powhatan. She probably saw white men for the first time in 1607 when English settlers landed at what was to become Jamestown, Virginia.

Pocahontas is believed to have performed an act of great courage in 1608. She may have saved the life of Captain John Smith just as he was about to be clubbed to death by her father's warriors.

Jamestown is now looked upon as the first permanent English settlement in North America. Pocahontas played a vital role in Jamestown's success. She helped supply the colonists with food. She warned Captain Smith of her father's plans that put his life in danger.

Pocahontas later married a colonist. To the English she became a symbol of the blending of the Native American and European cultures.

Much of what we know about Pocahontas comes from the efforts of John Smith. He wrote nearly a dozen books and reports about the English colonies in America.

William Strachey, a colonist, also wrote about Pocahontas. He arrived in Jamestown in 1610. He was the colony's historian. In a book he wrote about Virginia, he repeated stories about Pocahontas told to him by other colonists.

The books by Smith and Strachey are primary sources. In their efforts to learn about a person or the past, historians use both primary sources and secondary sources. Primary sources are actual records that have been handed down to us from former times.

A secondary source is a secondhand source. It is the description of an event by someone who did not witness the event.

A history textbook is a secondary source. So are the *World Book* and other encyclopedias. Modern magazine articles or books *about* Pocahontas are secondary sources.

There are many different types of primary sources, too. Books are merely the best known. Reports, diaries, speeches, letters, and poems that date to the time are primary sources.

Newspapers are also primary sources. So are painted portraits, business cards, marriage licenses, high school yearbooks, and movie tickets.

Thanks to a primary source, we have an idea of what Pocahontas looked like. A young Dutch artist named Simon Van de Passe sketched Pocahontas's portrait. She was in England at the time. She is dressed as an English noblewoman. Van de Passe's drawing was published in 1616. It has been copied and recopied countless times in the centuries since.

When working with a primary source, try to understand as much as you can about it.

When was it created? Why was it created?

For example, facts put forth by John Smith are sometimes questioned. He first told of being rescued by Pocahontas in 1624. Pocahontas was no longer living. Neither were any of the others involved in the rescue.

Smith had written of the colony earlier, in 1607.

This engraving of Pocahontas by Simon Van de Passe appeared in John Smith's Generall Historie of Virginia. *It is the only image of Pocahontas made during her lifetime.*

He told the story of his capture by the Powhatans. But he made no mention of the rescue.

Why did Smith wait so long to tell the story of being saved by Pocahontas?

Had he heard the tale from others? Was he merely repeating it to make a more colorful story? Or was it actual fact?

Nobody knows for sure.

None of the details of Pocahontas's life come from her own words. We have to look to John Smith, William Strachey, and others for this information. Sadly, they left some gaps in Pocahontas's story. We have to rely on historians to fill in the gaps. From these many sources, we are able to tell the story of Pocahontas and get a sense of what she was really like.

POWHATAN PRINCESS

OCAHONTAS WAS BORN IN 1595 OR 1596. She and her people were Powhatans. The Powhatans lived in the Chesapeake Bay area of what is now Virginia. They were made up of thirty different tribal groups. They had a total population of 14,000 to 15,000.

The Powhatans were an Algonkian-speaking people. The use of Algonkian was widespread. It could be heard as far north as Labrador, Canada, and even beyond. It was spoken in the Great Lakes region and in the Mississippi Valley.

The Powhatans were under the control of Wahunsonacock, Pocahontas's father. He was the "great king." He was called Powhatan after the settlement where he was born.

From his father, Powhatan inherited leadership of the village and other tribal groups. He later conquered many neighboring tribes. The people ruled by Powhatan became known as Powhatans.

John Smith described Powhatan as being tall and gray-haired. His age in 1608, Smith guessed, was "near sixtye [sixty]." Smith said the Supreme Chief had a "hardy body to endure any labor."

Powhatan ruled with a firm hand. William Strachey wrote of Powhatan, ". . . his will is lawe [law] and must be obeyed, not only as a king, but half as a god."

Powhatan had many wives. He also had as many as twenty sons and ten daughters.

Pocahontas was his favorite. John Smith described Pocahontas as Powhatan's "most deare [dear] and beloved daughter."

Pocahontas and her father lived in a village on the banks of what is now the York River. The village was called Werowocomoco. The site is probably about eleven miles downstream from the present West Point, Virginia.

In her preteen years, Pocahontas would have led a free and active life. Coastal Virginia offered bays, streams, and "chrystall [crystal] rivers" in which she could have waded and bathed. Like other Powhatan children, she would have learned to swim at a very early age.

Pocahontas would have been skilled in handling the Powhatan canoes. They were made of hollowed-out tree trunks. There were countless rivers and streams to be explored. The great Virginia forests were another

Pocahontas appears as a young woman in this engraving. However, she was only a child of eleven or twelve years old when the first English colonists arrived.

of her playgrounds. There were no enemies to fear. Except for an occasional bear, there were no dangerous animals.

Pocahontas probably would have gathered strawberries, raspberries, and mulberries in the woodlands. Cherries grew in big bunches. She and her friends would have filled their woven baskets with them. Walnuts, chestnuts, and hazelnuts were available, too.

Little girls of the tribe learned beadwork. They made dolls' clothes with beads.

The beads were made of shells. These were gathered along the riverbanks and the shore of the bay. The most prized shells were the spiral ones of small marine snails. These were used for trimming deerskin shirts and moccasins. Larger circular or oval shells were strung to be used as necklaces or bracelets.

The women were the tribe's house builders. A Powhatan house was made of a framework of young trees. The thicker ends were secured in the ground.

Powhatan dwellings were made of a framework of bent saplings (inset) over which strips of woven marsh grass were placed. The Jamestown Settlement offers this re-creation of one such home.

The thinner ends were bent to meet at the top. Then they were tied together with roots or strips of bark to form an arched structure.

The roof and sides of the house were made of mats woven from the stalks of marsh grass.

The women of the tribe also performed the household chores. They gathered and prepared the food. They cultivated the fields, collected wood, and hauled water. They tanned hides and stitched them into clothing.

Pocahontas, as the daughter of the Supreme Chief, escaped the hard work. She was likely pampered by her father's many wives.

There were Powhatan women to care for her hair, cutting it and oiling it. They adorned it with flowers and feathers.

As the daughter of a chief, Pocahontas would have been trained in the social graces of her people. Constant chatter was considered rude. She spoke carefully and deliberately. As a well-mannered person, she would pause between sentences. By pausing, she gave the listener a time for thought.

Children were taught to sit quietly beside their mothers.

"A child that cannot sit still is a half-developed child," one Powhatan leader said.

Good posture was very important. Pocahontas would have been taught how to stand up straight, with her shoulders back. Powhatan girls were sometimes made to sit for hours at a time with their backs against a wall to make them straight.

Powhatan and Pocahontas were very close. They were often together in his house. When he went out among his people, Pocahontas was at his side.

So Pocahontas would have been among the first to hear the exciting news. Three sailing ships had been sighted gliding up the James River. One was very large. The two others were smaller.

The ships carried white men. A Powhatan hunting party had watched as twenty or thirty men from the ships went ashore in a small boat. They wandered about, remaining until dark.

They never saw several Powhatans crawling toward them through the tall grass. Suddenly the Powhatans attacked. Their arrows filled the air. Two white men were wounded. When the strangers answered with gunfire, the Powhatans fled into the woods. None were harmed.

Powhatan soon learned of what had taken place. He decided to wait a few days before doing anything.

Pochins, one of Powhatan's sons, was in charge of a small village not far from where the ships were anchored. For the present, Powhatan would let Pochins keep an eye on the situation.

THE ENGLISH

THE POWHATANS WERE CURIOUS about the strangers. Why had they come? How long were they going to stay?

They kept a close watch on the visitors. They peered out at them from behind tree trunks or while hidden in tall grass.

The strangers were from England. There were 104 of them. They were all men.

They had arrived on three ships. The largest was the *Susan Constant*. The *Godspeed* and the *Discovery* were the other two.

The small fleet had been financed by a group of English investors. They called themselves the Virginia Company of London.

King James of England had granted the

The Susan Constant *was the largest of three vessels that brought the first English colonists to Virginia. It carried about fifty-four passengers and a twelve-man crew. This is a replica of the ship, on exhibition at the Jamestown Settlement.*

Virginia Company a charter, or certain rights, to form two colonies. One colony was North Virginia. This was later called New England. The other colony was called South Virginia. This included the coastal areas of what is now the state of Virginia.

The Virginia Company's three ships anchored in Chesapeake Bay on April 26, 1607. The difficult journey from England had taken eighteen weeks.

The English looked out upon the Virginia coast and were excited by what they saw. One of the colonists wrote of the "many sweet and delicate flowres [flowers] on the shore." He described the rivers "flowing through the Woods with great plentie [plenty] of fish of all kinds."

Near the mouth of the bay, a large river flowed. The colonists named it the James River, after King James I, England's ruler at the time.

The English sent exploring parties up the river in small boats. At a point where the James River met what is now known as the Chickahominy River, they found a site that seemed well suited for settlement.

It was a peninsula, a piece of land that extended out into the river. It was about two miles long and one mile wide. They named it Jamestown.

The English did not know that the land they looked out upon was Powhatan land. Even if they had known, it is not likely they would have cared. The English considered themselves superior to the Native Americans. They called them savages. How could savages own land?

Once their ships were anchored offshore, the English began setting up a temporary camp. This was quickly replaced by a walled settlement, a fort. It was triangular in shape, with the walls made of tall tree trunks. These were pointed at the top.

Within the fort, the settlers built a number of crude houses and a storehouse. The typical house was made of split logs coated with a mixture of mud and grass. Marsh reeds were used to thatch the roof.

The settlers devoted much of their energy to building a church. John Smith described it in his book. "Wee [we] did hang an old saile [sail] to three or foure [four] trees to shadow us from the Sunne

The typical Jamestown house, re-created at the Jamestown Settlement, was home to six to eight men, one of whom was the cook.

[the sun]. Our walls were rales [rails] of wood, our seats unhewed logs...our pulpit a bar of wood nailed to two neighboring trees."

Life was difficult for the English. About half of the first settlers were gentlemen. They were not used to doing physical labor. They counted on others to do it. As a result, many jobs never got done.

Captain Smith noted that some of the men "would rather starve and rot with idlenes [idleness], than be perswaded [persuaded] to do anything for their owne [own] relief."

The colonists grew corn, squash, and beans, but only in small amounts. They did not grow nearly enough to feed themselves. They hoped to trade with the Powhatans for corn and meat.

One day in May 1607, about 100 Powhatans approached the fort. They were armed with bows and arrows. They brought with them "a Fat Deare [deer]" as a gift. The Powhatans invited the settlers to join in a feast.

All went well at first. Then a Powhatan tribesman picked up a hatchet. Such tools were unknown to the Powhatans. The man may only have wanted to examine it. Nevertheless, the English grabbed their rifles and swords.

The Powhatans "went suddenly away...in great anger." As they stalked out of the fort, they promised revenge.

They kept their promise. Late in May, a force of some 200 Powhatans attacked. Many settlers were working outside the fort when the Powhatans struck. They had no chance to resist. For a time it appeared that the Powhatan bows and arrows would overwhelm the settlers. But then the English opened fire with the ships' cannons. The "huge noise" frightened the Powhatans. They fled into the forest.

Several Powhatans were killed. Many others were wounded. An English boy was killed during the attack. Another settler later died of wounds he had received.

Once work on the fort was finished, the Powhatans kept a watchful eye on it. They were careful to stay beyond the range of English rifles.

Early in the summer, the Powhatans saw the two largest English ships sail away. They were returning to England for supplies.

The Powhatans were anxious to know where the ships had gone. One of Powhatan's brothers

Jamestown's houses and other buildings were enclosed within a triangular-shaped fort. The fort's walls were made of tall tree trunks that were pointed at the top.

delivered a deer to the fort. His men asked what had happened to the ships. They are "not far off," the men were told.

Then the Powhatans learned that many of the white men were starving and sick. They had nothing to eat but a small supply of wheat and some wormy barley. They were afraid to leave the fort to hunt or fish. Some grew sick from drinking salty water from their shallow wells. One after another, the settlers were dying.

The English did not want the Powhatans to know the colony was being weakened by the deaths. "Do not advertize [advertise] the killing of any of your men, so that the country people may know it." These were the instructions they had received from the Virginia Company. Graves were dug during the dark of night. Burials were conducted in secret.

Meanwhile the Powhatans were celebrating. It was harvest time. The corn had ripened. There was squash, pumpkin, and turkey.

Since they had more than enough for themselves, the Powhatans decided to trade. The settlers welcomed them. In return for corn and other food, the English gave the Powhatans a few hatchets, bells, glass beads, and bits of copper.

Within a few weeks, the Powhatans' food supply began to dwindle. They had no more corn to trade. It became obvious to the settlers that they needed new trading partners. They would have to travel farther inland to find them.

In November 1607, a group of settlers made plans to venture up the Pamunkey River in small boats.

Their goal was to seek out Powhatan himself. By now, the English understood that Powhatan was the Supreme Chief. It was he with whom they would have to deal.

While some of the Powhatans were friendly toward the settlers, others were not. They wished to destroy the struggling colony. The English realized that the mission into unknown land could be very dangerous. John Smith wrote, "Lotts [lots] were cast [to decide] who should go."

Were dice rolled? Were straws drawn? Was a coin tossed? Smith did not say. Whatever method was used, it was Smith who was chosen. "...the chance was mine," he wrote.

CAPTURE AND RESCUE

CAPTAIN JOHN SMITH WAS THE right man to lead the mission. He was now twenty-seven years old. He had enjoyed an exciting career as a soldier and adventurer. His experiences had prepared him for the challenges he was about to face.

As a boy, Smith worked on his father's farm. He went to school until he was fifteen. Then he left home to become a soldier. He survived several daring adventures in western Europe. He later joined a Christian army to fight the Turks in Hungary.

Smith returned to England in 1604. He later wrote, "The Warres [wars] in Europe, Asia, and

Affrica [Africa] taught me how to subdue the wilde [wild] salvages [savages] . . . in America."

A short man with a thick beard, Smith was well known to the Powhatans. He had traded with them several times. Smith was known as a skilled trader. But he was a fair one. He was a man of his word. The Powhatans respected him.

In December 1607, Smith and fifteen men in two boats made their way up the Chickahominy River. The party included two Powhatan guides. Smith's goal was to make contact with Powhatan. He hoped to trade copper, beads, and other trinkets for food.

Before long, the river became too shallow for Smith's boat. Some of the men went ashore. Smith took one of the Powhatan guides and set out to explore the area.

Smith had not gone far before a Powhatan hunting party spotted him. One of the Powhatans fired an arrow. It struck Smith in the thigh but bounced off without doing any harm.

Two other Powhatans reached for their bows and arrows. Smith fired his musket at them.

John Smith's bold leadership helped Jamestown to survive. He later wrote several books about the colony.

Other Powhatans closed in on him. Smith grabbed his guide. He held the man in front of him with one hand. He held his musket in the other.

Powhatans surrounded Smith. Those closest to him got ready to release their arrows. But the man that Smith was using as a shield cried out. He told the hunters to put down their arrows. This man is a white chief, he said. He has great power.

The Powhatans could not kill a chief on the spur of the moment. Certain rules had to be followed.

The Powhatans announced they would lay down their weapons. But they wanted Smith to give up his musket. The captain refused.

Still holding the Powhatan guide in front of him, Smith backed slowly away. Perhaps he was hoping to make a quick break for his boat, which was nearby.

But instead Smith backed into a swampy patch of ground. A "bogmire," he called it. Smith fell into the soft mud. His guide went down with him. Smith then had no choice but to surrender. He would "trie [try] their mercies," as he put it.

The Powhatans released the guide and marched Smith to his boat. Other Powhatans had built a fire not far from the riverbank. A white man lay dead before it. Smith recognized the man as Jehu Robinson, a member of his party. He had "20 or 30 arrowes [arrows] in him," Smith noted.

Once Smith had warmed himself by the fire, he asked to be set free. The Powhatans said nothing. Smith asked to see their chief. They agreed to arrange the meeting.

Smith then took the opportunity to try to impress the Powhatans with a bit of magic. He took his compass from his pocket and showed them how it worked. They were awed by the instrument.

Smith described the moment in these words: "Much they marvailed [marveled] at the playing of the...Needle, which they could see so plainely [plainly], and yet not touch it, because of the glasse [glass] that covered [it]."

In the weeks that followed, the Powhatans marched their captive from one village to another. Smith met many tribal chiefs. Native priests danced and chanted before him.

Not long before dawn one bitter cold day late in December 1607, Smith and his captors were led to a rise above the river. A great number of Powhatan dwellings had been built there. They had arrived at Werowocomoco, the village that served as the official seat of the Powhatan government.

It was likely that no white person had ever seen the village. It was one of the largest of all Powhatan settlements. Werowocomoco was made up of about 100 homes with domelike roofs. They were

Historians do not agree exactly where in Virginia Werowocomoco was located, but John Smith described the site as being on the York River.

sprinkled across some two acres of fields. Corn, beans, and tobacco were grown there.

Some of the larger houses were rectangular in shape. They were called longhouses.

One of the longhouses was the biggest building that Captain Smith had ever seen in Virginia. It was about sixty feet long. The interior had been divided into several chambers. This was Powhatan's longhouse.

Powhatan knew that Smith was coming. He was waiting for him. Pocahontas was at his side.

Once inside the longhouse, Smith was paraded before 200 of Powhatan's warriors. They glared at him. "Grim Courtiers," Smith called them. When he came face-to-face with the Supreme Chief, "all the people gave a great shout."

Smith described the scene: Powhatan sat "before a fire upon a seat like a bedstead...covered with a great robe made of Rarowcun [raccoon] skins." On each side of the house there were "two rowes [rows] of men, and behind them as many women, with all their heads and shoulders painted red" and with "many of their heads bedecked with the white downe [down] of birds...a great chayne [chain] of white beads about their necks."

Women approached Smith bringing water. By nods and gestures, Smith was instructed to wash his hands. It was the custom for Powhatans to do this before a meal.

Another woman came forward after Smith had washed his hands. She "brought him a bunch of feathers, instead of a Towell [towel] to dry them."

The Powhatans then feasted. After, Powhatan called for a conference with his advisers.

Smith, writing in 1624, described what happened after the meeting ended. Powhatan ordered "two great stones" to be brought before him. Smith was then dragged forward and made to place his head on one of the stones. Two Powhatans stood over Smith with raised clubs, "ready... to beate [beat] out his braines [brains]."

Smith was ready to take his last breath. Suddenly he felt a slim body slam against his own. It was young Pocahontas.

She had thrown herself down and got Smith's "head in her armes [arms] and laid her owne [own] upon his to save him from death."

The ceremony was halted. Smith could go free.

Pocahontas's rescue of John Smith is one of the most often repeated tales in American history.

King Powhatan comands C: Smith to be slayne,

Pocahontas begs for John Smith's life. This version of the event appears in Smith's Generall Historie of Virginia.

But the meaning of the ceremony has been debated. Some historians say that Powhatan had no intention of executing Smith. He was only pretending in order to test Smith's courage. If Smith showed any sign of fear, he would have failed the test. He would have been considered a coward.

Other historians say that Smith had taken part in a Powhatan adoption ceremony. No execution had been staged. No rescue had actually taken place. What had happened was meant to symbolize the end of Smith's present life and the beginning of a new one as a member of Powhatan's tribe.

Some early historians said that Smith made up the tale. But it is now widely believed that Smith's account of what happened is factual.

One thing is certain: After the rescue, a special bond came to exist between Pocahontas and John Smith.

In addition, Pocahontas took on a new role. She began acting as a messenger for her father in his relations with the Jamestown settlers. As such, she would, in John Smith's words, help to preserve the colony "from death, famine, and utter confusion."

GIFTS FOR
POWHATAN

TWO DAYS AFTER BEING SAVED BY Pocahontas, Captain Smith was taken to a "great house in the woods." There he was left alone in a room where a fire was burning.

Before long, Smith heard mournful chanting. What did it mean? Smith had no idea.

Suddenly Powhatan appeared. His body had been painted black. A crowd of warriors followed him. They also were painted black.

Powhatan told the captain that he was now his adopted son. Pocahontas was now Smith's sister. Powhatan was father to them both.

Powhatan also announced that Smith was now a chief. Like all the other chiefs, Smith was to give him gifts. What he wanted, Powhatan said, were "two greate [great] guns" [cannons] and a millstone for grinding corn.

Smith could now go back to Jamestown. Rawhunt, a trusted aid of Powhatan's, and a party of twelve guards would go with him. The guards would bring back the gifts.

Once they arrived at Jamestown, Smith showed the guards the cannons. Each weighed from 3,000 to 4,000 pounds. They could not be moved. The same with the millstone. It was too heavy to move.

As substitutes for the cannons and millstone, Smith gave the Powhatans what he called "toyes" [toys]. These included bells, glass trinkets, and small pieces of copper that had been made into jewelry.

Not long after the Powhatans left, the *Susan Constant*, captained by Christopher Newport, arrived back in Jamestown. The ship brought almost 100 new colonists. The vessel also brought, in John Smith's words, "all things [that] could

In his dealings with the Powhatans, Captain Smith was firm but fair. The Powhatans respected him.

be imagined necessary for both [the newcomers] and for us."

"All things" included clothing, farming equipment, guns, and ammunition. In addition, the ship carried a supply of English food. The settlers feasted on beef, pork, and cheese.

On January 7, 1608, five days after the arrival of the *Susan Constant*, disaster struck. A fire swept through Jamestown. The flames leapt from one straw-roofed house to the next. The church and storehouse were burned to the ground. Only three small buildings were saved. Jamestown was all but destroyed.

The colonists had talked earlier of abandoning the settlement and returning to England. Now such talk was heard again.

Powhatan came to the colonists' rescue. When he heard of the tragic fire, he ordered that food be brought to the settlement. Powhatans arrived "every other day," Smith wrote, and "brought . . . bread, fish, turkies [turkeys], squirrels, deare [deer], and other wild beasts."

Pocahontas went along with the tribesmen who delivered the food. She and Captain Smith were beginning to be able to talk with one another. Smith had been working hard to learn Algonkian. Pocahontas had helped him. Under her guidance, he had learned to convert Algonkian words into English. He kept a notebook in which he wrote down the words that he wanted to learn. In time, Smith could speak long sentences in the language.

He once sent a message to Pocahontas. He first wrote down the words in Algonkian. Beneath them he wrote the English translation: "Bid Pocahontas bring hither two little Baskets and I will give her white Beads to make her a Chaine [chain]."

Toward the end of February in 1608, Captain Newport had a request for Captain Smith. He asked to be taken to Werowocomoco to meet Powhatan. The Supreme Chief sent word that he would welcome him. As soon as the weather permitted, Smith and Newport set out. They took about forty well-armed men with them.

When they arrived at Powhatan's longhouse, they

Becaufe many doe defire to know the manner of their Language, I haue inferted thefe few words.

KA katorswines yowo. What call you this.

Nemarough, a man.

Crenepo, a woman.

Marowancheffo, a boy.

Tchawkans, Houfes.

Matchcores, Skins, or garments.

Mockafins, Shooes.

Tuffan, Beds. *Pokatawer,* Fire.

Attawp, A bow. *Attonce,* Arrowes.

Monacookes, Swords.

Aumoubhowgh, A Target.

Pawcuffacks, Gunnes.

Tomahacks, Axes.

Tockahacks, Pickaxes.

Pamefacks, Kniues.

Accowprets, Sheares.

Pawpecones, Pipes. *Mattaffin,* Copper

Vffawaffin, Iron, Braffe, Silver, or any white mettall. *Muffes,* Woods.

Attaffkuff, Leaues, weeds, or graffe.

Chepfin, Land. *Shacquohocan.* A ftone.

Wepenter, A cookold.

Suckahanna, Water. *Noughmaff,* Fifh.

Copotone, Sturgeon.

Weghfhaughes, Flefh.

Sawwehone, Bloud.

Netoppew, Friends.

Marrapough, Enemies.

Maskapow, the worft of the enemies.

Mawchick chammay, The beft of friends

Cafacunnakack, peya quagh acquintan vttafantafough, In how many daies will there come hither any more Englifh Ships.

Their Numbers.

Necut, 1. *Ningh,* 2. *Nuff,* 3. *Yowgh,* 4. *Paranske,* 5. *Comotinch,* 6. *Toppawoff,* 7 *Nuffwafh,* 8. *Kekatawgh,* 9. *Kaskeke* 10 They count no more but by tennes as followeth.

Cafe, how many.

Ningbfapooekiku, 20.

Nuffapooeksku, 30.

Yowghapooeksku, 40.

Parankeftaffapooekfku, 50.

Comatinchtaffapooekfku, 60.

Nuffwafhtaffatpooekfku, 70.

Kekataughtaffapooekfku, 90.

Necuttoughtyfinough, 100.

Necuttweunquaough, 1000.

Rawcofowghs, Dayes.

Kefkowghes, Sunnes.

Toppquongh. Nights.

Nepawwefhowghs, Moones.

Pawpaxfoughes, Yeares.

Pummahumps, Starres.

Ofies, Heavens.

Okees, Gods.

Quiyougbcofoughs, Pettie Gods, and their affinities.

Righcomoughes, Deaths.

Kekughes, Liues.

Mowchick woyawgh tawgh noeragh kaquere mecher, I am very hungry? what fhall I eate?

Tawnor nehiegh Powhatan, Where dwels Powhatan.

Atache, nehiegh yourewgh, Orapaks. Now he dwels a great way hence at Orapaks.

Vittapitchewayne anpcchitchs nehawper Werowacomoco, You lie, he ftaid ever at Werowacomoco.

Kator nehiegh mattagh neer vtt pit-chewayne, Truely he is there I doe not lie.

Spaughtynere keragh werowance maw-marinough k. kate wawgh peyaquaugh, Run you then to the King Mawma-rynough and bid him come hither.

Vtteke, e peya weyack wighn hip, Get you gone, & come againe quickly.

Kekaten Pokahontas patiaquagh niugh tanks manotyens neer mowchick raw-renock audowgh, Bid Pokahontas bring hither two little Baskets, and I will giue her white Beads to make her a Chaine.   *FINIS.*

Captain Smith made a great effort to learn Algonkian, the Powhatan language. In his Generall Historie of Virginia, *he offered this list of Algonkian words and terms with the English translation for each.*

saw forty or fifty platters of bread outside it. That was a sign that the visitors would be warmly received.

Newport and Smith brought gifts for Powhatan. They presented the Supreme Chief with a red wool suit, an English gentleman's hat, and a white greyhound. Powhatan loved dogs. He had never seen a greyhound before. The tall and slender animal delighted him.

Powhatan proclaimed everlasting friendship with the colonists. To seal his declaration, the Supreme Chief proposed that he and the English follow a Powhatan custom and exchange hostages. Powhatan presented the English with one of his trusted servants, a young boy named Namontack. In return, the English gave over thirteen-year-old Thomas Savage to Powhatan. Each of the young men was to adapt to his new culture. Once he had learned the language, he was to act as an interpreter.

Several days of feasting and dancing followed. The Powhatans and the colonists also traded.

As a trader, Captain Newport was very generous with Powhatan. Too generous, in fact. For a small amount of corn, Newport gave the Supreme Chief twelve copper kettles. This upset Captain Smith. He realized that Newport's generosity could soon starve the colony.

But Captain Smith helped to restore the balance between the trading partners. He had brought with him a supply of beads of blue Venetian glass. Smith flashed the sparkling beads before Powhatan and his tribesmen. They had never seen anything like them before.

The beads were, Smith later recalled, "the colour of the skyes [skies]...a most rare substance." They were "not to be worne [worn] but by the greatest kings in the world."

Powhatan and his tribesmen were in awe. They gladly traded more than 200 bushels of corn for a few pounds of the beautiful glass beads, which had little value.

Captain Smith had made up for Newport's mistakes. But Newport continued to let himself be out-traded by the Powhatans. On April 10, 1608, Captain Newport sailed for England aboard the

Susan Constant. Before he left, Powhatan sent the captain a gift of twenty wild turkeys. He asked Newport to send him twenty English swords in return. Newport did.

This angered Captain Smith. Newport had again allowed Powhatan to get the better of him.

By now, spring was at hand. The planting season had begun. The Powhatans continued to be friendly.

Native trading parties visited the fort. Pocahontas came with them. She soon became friendly with several English boys. They often played together, performing somersaults and cartwheels.

Pocahontas enjoyed the company of John Smith on her visits. He was her special friend.

Later, Powhatan sent another gift of twenty turkeys to the colony. Again, he asked for twenty swords in return.

Captain Smith refused. Thanks to Newport, the Powhatans already had too many swords, Smith believed. Besides, he had none to spare. He would give them bells and beads, but no swords.

From dealing with Newport, the Powhatans were

To painter Robert Matthew Sully, Pocahontas was "a forest girl." In the 1850s, he painted her with a crown and a regal cloak.

used to getting their own way. They wanted swords. If Smith would not give swords to them, they would take them. They began trying to steal swords at the fort. They also made off with axes, shovels, and muskets. They would sometimes surprise colonists outside the fort and take their swords from them.

One day a handful of Powhatans ambushed Captain Smith. They tried to get his sword. Smith was quick to react. Taking some men from the fort, Smith captured seven Powhatans. He imprisoned them within the fort.

Then the Powhatans captured two colonists. The next thing Smith knew, a group of Powhatans had assembled outside the fort. They demanded that Smith release the seven Powhatan prisoners. If he refused, there would be trouble.

John Smith was not a man to be bullied. Led by Smith, a party of colonists went on a rampage through nearby Powhatan villages, setting them ablaze. Before the day was over, the two colonists held captive had been returned. And the Powhatans were asking for peace.

Shortly after, Powhatan sent Pocahontas to Jamestown to seek to get the Powhatan captives released. Rawhunt went with her. He was Powhatan's most trusted messenger. Rawhunt "told mee [me]," Smith wrote, "how well Powhatan loved and respected mee..."

Smith agreed to let the prisoners go. But he made it clear he was doing it for Pocahontas. It was because of her, and her alone, that the prisoners had gained their life and liberty.

TROUBLE IN JAMESTOWN

With the return of the Powhatan captives, peace settled upon Jamestown. Captain Smith took advantage of the calm to do some exploring.

Traveling by boat, Smith set sail from the fort late in the spring of 1608. He took fourteen men with him. Their goal was to scout and survey the vast Chesapeake Bay area.

Smith and his men sailed up the Potomac River. They traveled about as far as the present city of Washington, D.C. They nudged their way into shallow inlets. They followed narrow creeks. Smith made maps of the region. He gave names to the rivers and streams.

Captain John Smith's carefully drawn map of the region surrounding Chesapeake Bay.

On any trail they blazed, the men hacked crosses into trees. This was "to signify to any [that] Englishmen had been there."

Smith and his companions came upon several Native Americans who did not speak Algonkian. Smith used sign language to communicate with them.

Only animals populated some areas. Smith

reported seeing woods "...full of Woolves [wolves], Beares [bears], Deare [deer], and other wild beastes [beasts]."

The marshlands were also rich in wildlife. Smith and his men saw otter, beaver, mink, martin, and sable. Fish were thick in the water. The men tried catching them in frying pans.

Captain Smith speared fish with his sword. One day as he was struggling to remove a dangerous stingray from his sword tip, the creature plunged its bony spine into his wrist. The poison worked fast. The captain's hand and arm swelled up.

But in the end, Smith got the better of the stingray. He reported that he was well enough by nightfall to "eate [eat] the fish for supper."

When Smith and his men returned to Jamestown that summer, they were greeted as heroes. Smith was elected governor of the colony a few days after their arrival.

Smith demanded order and discipline in Jamestown. Every Saturday, the men were made to drill in military fashion outside the fort. Sometimes as many as 100 Powhatans would watch in wide-eyed wonder.

Smith put men to work repairing the church. A new roof was put on the storehouse.

Smith had been governor of the colony for about a month when Captain Newport returned from another voyage to England. He brought about eighty new settlers with him. They included the first two women.

He also brought orders that disturbed Smith. The directors of the Virginia Company wanted Powhatan to be crowned as a king. They had even sent a copper crown and a red robe to be used for the coronation ceremony.

The English thought that the crowning would make Powhatan a loyal subject of the English. The Supreme Chief would then be obedient and easy to govern.

But Smith thought the plan was nonsense. Powhatan didn't need the English to make him a king. He was already a king. Smith felt the plan could backfire. Powhatan could be offended by the plan. He might even become hostile again.

Smith wrote to the directors of the Virginia Company. "By whose advice you sent him [Powhatan] such presents, I know not," Smith said. "But this gives me leave to tell you, I fear there will be [trouble for us all before] we hear from you again."

While Smith did not like the Virginia Company's orders, he could not ignore them. He and a party of four went to Werowocomoco with the idea of inviting Powhatan to come to Jamestown for the coronation. Powhatan was away on a hunting expedition when they arrived.

Pocahontas was there to greet Smith and his companions instead. She and some thirty of her friends decided to entertain the visitors. They painted their bodies and danced for them. They sang to music provided by drums, flutes, and rattles. "When they sing," wrote William Strachey, "they have a delightful and pleasant tang to their voices."

The next day, Powhatan returned. When Captain Smith invited him to Jamestown to be crowned a king, Powhatan reacted just as Smith thought he would react. "I will not bite at such bait," Powhatan said. "I also am a King, and this is my land. Your father [Captain Newport] is to come to me, not I to him..."

Smith returned to Jamestown to report that the coronation must take place in Werowocomoco. Captain Newport, with seventy men, sailed from Jamestown to the Powhatan settlement. Smith, taking another fifty men, marched to the settlement.

Once the coronation ceremony began, the English presented gifts to Powhatan. He received a bed complete with bedding, a wide-spouted pitcher, a basin, and the scarlet coat.

But when it came time for him to kneel to receive the crown, Powhatan refused. He would not even bow his head. Finally, several settlers pushed down his shoulders, making him stoop slightly. Newport quickly set the copper crown upon his head.

Powhatan knew that he was now expected to give

Powhatan was unwilling to take part in the coronation ceremony staged by the English. He realized that they were seeking to make him a subject of their king.

gifts to the English in return for the crown. Newport leaned forward in anticipation. But all he got was an old pair of moccasins and a long deerskin cloak that Powhatan had been wearing. Powhatan also offered the English a few bushels of corn.

The English had been expecting Powhatan to be much more generous. But by his stinginess

Powhatan was sending a message. Powhatan was weary of the English. It was not merely the coronation ceremony. It was now plain to him that the English planned to stay in Virginia. Their settlement was a permanent one. And it was swelling in size. Once the Powhatans were superior in numbers to the English. Before very long, the English would outnumber the Powhatans. No wonder Chief Powhatan was upset.

After Captains Smith and Newport had left Werowocomoco, Powhatan told his people that they were to cease trading with the settlers. As for Pocahontas, she could no longer visit the Jamestown settlement.

Captain Smith was outraged when he learned that the Powhatans would no longer trade with the English. Where would the colony get corn and other food? Smith believed that it "was Powhatan's policy to starve us." He was prepared to fight for the food that the colony needed.

Then, unexpectedly, Powhatan sent messengers to Jamestown. They instructed Smith to visit him.

Powhatan promised to fill one of the English sailing ships with corn. In return, Powhatan wanted the English to build him a house like the ones in Jamestown. He also wanted a grindstone, fifty swords, some guns, beads, copper jewelry, a rooster, and a hen.

Smith accepted the invitation to visit. He first sent four men ahead to start building the house for Powhatan. Smith himself and forty-six volunteers sailed for Werowocomoco later in December 1608. Fierce blizzards and a river that was frozen in some places delayed them. They did not arrive until January 12, 1609.

The next day, Powhatan said he was ready to trade. But he wanted swords and guns, not beads and bells.

Smith said he had no swords or guns to spare. Then he issued a warning. He said that if Powhatan did not provide him with the help he was seeking, he might "dissolve that friendship [that] we have mutually promised." Smith was suggesting war.

Powhatan understood. The Supreme Chief

At Jamestown, the colony's original site, this statue honors Captain Smith, the colony's governor from 1608–1609.

agreed to give Smith eighty bushels of corn for a copper kettle. To Powhatan, a kettle was especially valuable. His people had no metal containers in which to boil liquids or cook food.

Smith got ready to load his ship and return to Jamestown. But he had to wait until the bushels of corn were brought from nearby villages. He also had to get some Powhatans to break the ice offshore. Otherwise, his vessel could not get close enough to be loaded.

During the delay, Powhatan slipped away. Shortly after, a number of his warriors surrounded his longhouse, still occupied by Smith and his men.

It didn't take Smith long to realize that they were now prisoners. With his sword in one hand and his pistol in the other, Smith bolted for the doorway. Warriors tried to block his exit. Smith fired his pistol. The Powhatans fled.

Powhatan's plot had failed. As if to apologize, the Supreme Chief sent Smith a pearl bracelet and a necklace.

Meanwhile, the baskets of corn had been loaded

aboard Smith's ship. But the river was at low tide. The ship could not sail. He and his men would have to spend the evening at Werowocomoco, waiting for the tide to change.

They sought out one of the empty longhouses at the settlement. Darkness had fallen. Smith and his men were restless, eager to return.

Suddenly, out of the night, Pocahontas slipped into the longhouse. Smith had not seen her that day. He thought she had gone away with her father. He could see that she was filled with anxiety.

Leave, she told Smith. Go immediately. Her father's warriors were going to try to kill him and his men.

Smith tried to give Pocahontas gifts. She refused them. If she were seen with gifts from the English, her father would have her killed. Then Pocahontas turned and left. It would be eight years before she and Captain Smith would see each other again.

TURNING POINT

I N THE MORNING, SMITH AND HIS men left Werowocomoco. But instead of sailing for Jamestown, they headed upriver. Smith wanted to trade for more corn. He planned to seek out Powhatan's brother Opechancanough.

Smith spent two days in Opechancanough's village before the Powhatan leader would talk of trade. But after Opechancanough sold Smith what corn he had, he tricked him. He lured Smith to his longhouse. Several hundred Powhatans then surrounded it.

Smith was equal to the situation. He rallied his men. "Let us fight like men, and not die like sheepe [sheep]!" he declared.

Outside the longhouse, Captain Smith seized Opechancanough by the long lock of hair he wore. He jammed his pistol into his ribs. He then forced the Powhatan leader to help him load the bushels of corn onto the ship.

When the corn was loaded, Smith paid for it with trade goods. "Whatsoever we gave them, they seemed well contented," Smith wrote.

When Smith returned to Jamestown, he brought corn enough to last through the winter. But to make it last, he established a new rule. No one would eat who did not work.

And Smith provided plenty of work. The church was given a new roof. Twenty new houses were built. A well was dug within the fort. A heavily fortified structure was built where the Jamestown peninsula met the mainland. The blockhouse, as it was called, was to serve as a checkpoint for Native American visitors.

Most importantly, Smith persuaded the settlers to be more serious about farming the land. "Thirty or forty acres of land we digged and planted," he wrote.

A nineteenth-century artist offered this version of Captain Smith's encounter with Opechancanough. His warriors bow down to the mighty English leader.

Early in July 1609, the struggling colonists were cheered by the sight of an English sailing ship approaching up the river. It carried 180 passengers. By nightfall, Jamestown's population had more than doubled.

Captain Samuel Argall was the commanding officer of the ship. He brought the news that seven other ships were on the way to Virginia. They would be bringing more than 500 new colonists.

During August, the ships arrived. Jamestown was not big enough to hold all the new settlers. Captain Smith arranged for many of the newly arrived men and women to settle in an abandoned Native American village. A son of Powhatan and his followers had once occupied the site. It was on the James River, downstream from Jamestown.

Smith and Powhatan's son made a deal. The English could have the village. In return, they would give Powhatan's son a supply of English copper. Smith also pledged English military support against the Monacans, a tribe from the west. The Monacans frequently raided Powhatan villages.

The new settlers had no talent for getting along with the Powhatans. They thought the Powhatans were inferior. They acted viciously against them. The Powhatans responded with cruelties of their own.

Late in August, Captain Smith went back to the new village. While there, he tried to settle a dispute between the settlers and the Powhatans.

While returning to Jamestown, Smith was the victim of a freak accident. He was napping in the bottom of his boat. The small deerskin bag in which he held his gunpowder hung from his waist. Suddenly a spark, perhaps from a crew member's pipe, ignited the powder, and it burst into flame.

The explosion left Smith horribly injured. It "tore the flesh from his body and thighes [thighs] . . . in a most pitifull [pitiful] manner." He jumped into the river to stop the burning.

Crew members aboard the boat rescued Smith from drowning and took him back to the fort. For days, his life hung in the balance.

Smith survived and his wounds began to heal. He

eventually was able to turn his attention back to the colony. He found that his stern rule was being challenged. Some of the settlers were seeking a new governor.

Smith was worn out. He did not want to become involved in a struggle to retain leadership. His injury needed better treatment than was available in Jamestown. Sometime during September 1609, Smith boarded a ship bound for England. After more than two years in Virginia, he was returning home.

Smith sent no message to Pocahontas telling her of his departure. Word reached her through her people that Captain Smith was no longer present at Jamestown. Some people said he had sailed away in one of the ships. Others said that he had died.

Pocahontas did not know. She made up her mind, however, never to set foot in Jamestown again. No longer would she help the colonists.

THE STARVING
TIME

IN THE YEARS THAT FOLLOWED CAPTAIN
John Smith's departure for London, little is
known of Pocahontas's life. There is almost
no record of her activities.

From time to time, however, her name would
be heard. In about the year 1610, "...young
Pocahunta [Pocahontas]," wrote William
Strachey, "is now married to a private Captayne
[captain] called Kocoum..."

Some historians believe that Kocoum was not
a Powhatan. He was possibly a Patawamake. The
Patawamakes lived to the north on the shores of
the Potomac River. Pocahontas was known to be
living among the Patawamakes by 1613.

For the Jamestown colony, these were years of great suffering and sorrow. Powhatan seemed more determined than ever to wipe out the English. Powhatan warriors lay in ambush night and day. Any Englishman caught outside the Jamestown fort was murdered.

At the same time, the colony was desperate for food. A trading mission of about thirty men headed up the Pamunkey River. The Powhatans lured them from their boat, then attacked them. All of the colonists were killed.

Jamestown's colonists were so desperate for food that they ate their farm animals. These were described as "Hogs, Hens, Goats, Sheepe [sheep], [and] Horse." Dogs and cats were eaten, too. Even mice and rats went into the pot. The Starving Time, it was called.

Within the fort, sickness and disease were widespread. At night, the English slipped outside to dig graves and hold brief burial ceremonies.

Almost ninety percent of the colonists died that winter. When Smith left Jamestown, the colony's

At Jamestown, this memorial cross has been erected to mark some of the
300 graves dug by the settlers during the winter of 1609–1610.

population was around 500. Six months after his departure, "there remained not past sixtie [sixty] men, women, and children, most miserable and poor creatures."

By mid-May 1610, those who had managed to survive the winter faced almost certain death. If starvation did not take them, a final Powhatan assault would.

But on May 23 that year, the colony's nightmare abruptly ended. In what the settlers believed to be an act of God, a pair of English sailing ships were sighted off Jamestown. They were aptly named the *Deliverance* and the *Patience*.

The two vessels carried about 100 passengers. These were men and women who had set sail from England almost a year before on the *Sea Venture*. Six other ships accompanied the *Sea Venture*. The fleet's mission was to resupply the Virginia colony.

The *Sea Venture* had met great misfortune. A ferocious hurricane separated the *Sea Venture* from the other vessels. The ship ended up on a Bermuda beach, a wreck. The passengers, however, managed to get ashore safely.

Using wood salvaged from the *Sea Venture* and Bermuda cedar, the survivors built two smaller ships. These ships were the *Deliverance* and *Patience*. Early in May 1610, they boarded the ships and set out again for Virginia.

When they arrived, they could not believe their eyes. They had expected to find a thriving community. What they saw was a disaster. Huge gaps had been ripped in the fence surrounding the fort. Gates were off their hinges. Houses were empty or had been burned to the ground. The people they saw seemed on the brink of death from starvation.

The settlement's leaders realized that the situation was hopeless. They agreed to abandon the colony and return to England.

June 7, 1610, was set as the day of departure. Anything worth keeping was loaded onto the *Deliverance* and *Patience*. Then the colonists went aboard. The two ships headed down the James River toward the open sea. It seemed that England's attempt to colonize the New World had ended.

Near the mouth of the James River, the ships dropped anchor. At daybreak, they would begin their Atlantic crossing.

The *Deliverance* and *Patience* were still at anchor early the next morning. Then crew members saw the outline of a huge sailing ship edging upstream toward them. It was the *De La Warre* from London. Two other ships were just behind the *De La Warre*. The *Deliverance* and *Patience* were ordered to reverse course and head back to Jamestown.

In the weeks that followed, the colony revived. The ships from England had brought food and supplies. The church was rebuilt and made larger. Homes were repaired. Fields were plowed and planted.

There would still be food shortages. The Powhatans would still be hostile. But Jamestown had been given a second chance.

THE PLOT

O N MAY 12, 1611, SIR THOMAS Dale arrived in Jamestown with a fleet of three ships. Dale was a military man, a veteran of foreign wars. He had been ordered to take command of the colony.

A year had passed since the arrival of the *De La Warre*. Dale found the colonists heading toward ruin again. They had "not put Corne [corn] in the ground for their bread." And "their homes [were] ready to fall on their heads."

Dale flew into a rage. He quickly began making changes.

He installed a harsh set of laws. He demanded strict obedience to them. "Lawes [laws] of blood," the colonists called them.

Swearing was forbidden. The first time a man was heard swearing, he was to be whipped. The second, he was to have his tongue pierced by a bodkin, a sharp pointed instrument. Swearing a third time could mean death.

If a man was caught picking grapes without permission, he could have his ears cut off.

Two women who sewed for the colonists were publicly whipped. Their crime: They had made men's shirts too short.

Dale had the same harsh attitude toward the natives. In a show of force, he led 100 heavily armed colonists against the Nansemonds, another Powhatan tribal group. These English wore armor. Dale had brought suits of armor from England.

Most Nansemonds had never seen men covered in metal before. When their arrows glanced off the armor, they were shocked. They tried chants and spells to stop the English. They called for rain to fall and dampen the English gunpowder. Nothing worked.

The armored English burned Nansemond houses.

Sir Thomas Dale became Jamestown's military commander in 1611. A period of harsh rule followed.

They cut down their corn. And when the English left, they took prisoners with them.

Dale was ambitious. During the summer of 1611, he set out in search of another site on the James River where a major settlement could be built. Sailing about forty-five miles upstream from Jamestown, Dale came upon a tongue-shaped piece of land that jutted out into the river. That is where he would build the new town, he decided. He would call it Henrico, after Prince Henry. Prince Henry was the oldest son of King James.

Dale returned to Jamestown to organize a workforce. He put men to work chopping down trees for the lumber he needed. He kept brickmakers busy, too. In mid-September, Dale set out from Jamestown with 350 workers to begin the construction of Henrico.

Although the Powhatans kept Dale's men under almost daily attack, the village was soon completed.

Ralph Hamor, the colony's historian, later wrote a description of Henrico. "There is in the town three streets of well-framed houses, a hansome [handsome]

At Henrico, the James River twists and turns and becomes much narrower.

church ... storehouses, watch-houses [and] five fair Block-houses ..."

Henrico became a symbol for the English. It represented their wish to expand their control beyond Jamestown.

Powhatan's warriors remained a problem, however. They continued to attack the English almost without letup. The English knew that they would have to bring the Powhatans under control. Otherwise, they could not claim to be masters of their new nation.

With Sir Thomas Dale busy at Henrico, Sir Thomas Gates became Jamestown's new governor. Gates returned from London in 1612 to take command. He had arrived at Jamestown with "six tall Ships, with three hundred Men, an hundred Cattle, two hundred Hogs, and with all Manner of other Munition and Provision."

By now, Jamestown was bursting at the seams with more than 700 settlers. With so many people, it was obvious to all that there was not enough food to last through the winter.

Trading with the Powhatans would solve the problem. But they had no wish to trade with the English.

The Patawamakes offered a solution. The Patawamakes lived to the north, along the banks of the Potomac River. They had traded with the English before. Perhaps they would again.

In December 1612, Captain Samuel Argall sailed from Jamestown aboard the *Treasurer* to meet with the Patawamakes. The thirty-two-year-old Argall had visited them before. He had been successful in his dealings with them.

In 1612, Argall again found the Patawamakes friendly and easy to deal with. He returned to Jamestown with 1,100 bushels of corn.

Argall also brought back some exciting news. He learned that Pocahontas was living in the region. The Powhatan princess was seventeen now. She was no longer with her husband, Kocoum. She was living alone, "unknown to all but trusty Friends."

A secret plan began to form in Argall's mind. He would kidnap Pocahontas. He would hold her captive and bring her back to Jamestown.

Once Powhatan learned that the English were holding his daughter hostage, he would change his ways, Argall believed. The Supreme Chief would be happy to agree to a lasting peace.

The more that Argall thought about the idea, the

more excited he got. He made up his mind "to possess myself of her by any stratagem that I could use." As the spring of 1613 approached, Argall got ready to put his plot into action.

KIDNAPPED

IN APRIL 1613, CAPTAIN SAMUEL Argall sailed the *Treasurer* back up the Potomac River to meet with the Patawamakes. Corn was not on his mind this time. Pocahontas was. Argall was determined to return to Jamestown with Powhatan's daughter as his captive.

Captain Argall was shrewd and sly. He knew that he could not take Pocahontas by force. He would have to find some way to lure her aboard the *Treasurer*.

He also realized that he could not carry out the plot by himself. He would need help.

Argall had someone in mind. He had a friend

among the Patawamakes. His name was Japazaws. His brother was the chief of the Patawamakes.

Argall told Japazaws of his plan. At first, Japazaws opposed the idea. Then Argall told Japazaws that "if he did not betray Pocahontas into my hands, wee [we] will no longer be brothers nor friends."

That wasn't all. Argall knew that Japazaws and his wife liked English goods. Argall promised them a fine copper kettle if they would help him.

At first, Japazaws was unwilling to help. But eventually he decided to go along with the plot.

The next day, Japazaws went to see Pocahontas. He told her that there was an English ship anchored in the river. Would she like to come and see it? Japazaws's wife would meet her. The two women could go aboard the ship together.

Pocahontas didn't need any convincing. She wanted to go. After four years away from Jamestown, she seemed "desirous to renue [renew] her familiaritie [familiarity] with the English," according to Ralph Hamor, the colony's historian.

Once Pocahontas was aboard the *Treasurer*,

Argall showed her every courtesy. He took her on a tour of the vessel. Then he ordered supper for her.

After the meal, Pocahontas was escorted to a cabin on the ship. There she napped.

When Pocahontas awakened, she felt uneasy. She knew she shouldn't be aboard the English ship. She went on deck and found Japazaws and his wife. She asked to go ashore.

Argall came forward. He told Pocahontas that she was being held as a hostage. Her father, Argall explained, "had...eight of our Englishmen, many swords and other tools which he [had taken]..." He told Pocahontas that she would not be released until the English prisoners and stolen goods had been returned.

Argall allowed Japazaws and his wife to go ashore. When they left, they carried their copper kettle with them.

Pocahontas found herself alone with Captain Argall and the *Treasurer's* crew of sixty, all white men. She became "pensive and discontented," according to Argall.

At the time of her capture, Pocahontas was about seventeen, an attractive and graceful young woman. This statue of the Powhatan princess greets visitors at Jamestown.

But she had no reason to be fearful. The crew treated her more like a guest than a prisoner. She was given the gunner's cabin as a place to stay. Except for the captain's cabin, it was the best on the ship.

On April 13, 1613, Argall left the Patawamakes and sailed for Jamestown. Before his departure, he sent a messenger to Powhatan. The messenger was "to let him know that I had taken his Daughter." Argall wanted Powhatan to release the English prisoners he had taken. He ordered him to "send home the Englishmen whom he deteined [detained] in slaverie [slavery]." He also said he wanted the swords and guns that the Powhatans had taken. In addition, Argall asked for "a great quantitie [quantity] of Corne [corn]." If Powhatan did as he was asked, his daughter would be released.

Argall returned to Jamestown. When he arrived there, he turned Pocahontas over to Sir Thomas Gates and Sir Thomas Dale. They were the highest-ranking of the colonists. They would bargain with Powhatan.

Their demands were similar to Argall's. They wanted Powhatan to return the eight Englishmen he held as prisoners. They also wanted him to return the weapons he had taken. Most of all, they wanted Powhatan "for ever to be friends with us."

Powhatan did return seven of the prisoners. He also sent a canoe filled with corn. But he kept the guns and swords.

Gates and Dale were not satisfied. But nothing more was heard from Powhatan. Weeks went by, then months. Still no word.

At first, Pocahontas believed that she would be held captive for only a short time. She felt sure that her father would pay whatever ransom was demanded. Then she would go free. But Gates and Dale heard nothing from Powhatan.

Summer faded into fall. Fall became winter. Still no word. Pocahontas realized that her stay with the English was going to be a long one. She decided that she had better make the best of it.

CHAPTER 11

THE CAPTIVE

POCAHONTAS DID NOT REMAIN IN Jamestown for very long. She was taken upriver to Henrico. That was where Sir Thomas Dale had carved out a "new towne [town]" in the wilderness.

Henrico was better protected than Jamestown. In Henrico, there was much less chance that Pocahontas could be recaptured by the Powhatans.

At Henrico, the English began to transform Pocahontas into a "model Indian Princess." They wanted to make her a symbol of English success in the New World.

Pocahontas went to live at Rock Hall, a 100-acre farm. Rock Hall was the home of the

Reverend Alexander Whitaker. Whitaker was a Puritan clergyman.

Lady members of Reverend Whitaker's church taught Pocahontas to dress as Englishwomen dressed. She put on tight-waisted, billowing skirts over long petticoats. She traded in her soft moccasins for leather shoes.

At the same time, Pocahontas began receiving instruction in the Christian faith. She memorized the Lord's Prayer. She studied the Ten Commandments. She learned to follow church services in the English Book of Common Prayer.

Pocahontas was an excellent pupil. She seemed entirely comfortable moving from one culture to the other.

John Rolfe, an English planter in the Henrico area, helped to instruct Pocahontas. He spoke of "her desyre [desire] to be taught and instructed in the knowledge of God...."

Rolfe was a handsome man in his middle to late twenties. He was well educated. Little by little, he became very fond of Pocahontas.

Pocahontas is presented as a woman of style and grace in this well-known painting by Thomas Sully, a leading portrait painter of the 1800s.

In the spring of 1614, Pocahontas became a Christian. Her baptism is believed to have taken place in the "faire [fair] and handsome Church at Henrico." She was given the Christian name Rebecca.

By becoming a Christian, Pocahontas had begun to adapt to English ways. But in the months that followed, she was to take even bigger steps in replacing her old culture with the new.

CHAPTER 12

LOVE AND MARRIAGE

INSIDE THE HIGH-DOMED CAPITOL IN Washington, D.C., today's visitors gaze at an important painting. It is titled "The Baptism of Pocahontas." The painting is the work of American artist John Gadsby Chapman.

In the painting, Pocahontas is kneeling before the Reverend Alexander Whitaker. Reverend Whitaker conducted the baptism ceremony. Pocahontas is dressed in a flowing white robe.

John Rolfe is another principal figure in the painting. He stands behind Pocahontas in the foreground at the right.

Rolfe deserved an important place in the

Pocahontas's sister appears in John Gadsby Chapman's painting "The Baptism of Pocahontas." She is seated in the foreground and holds a baby.

painting. Within a month or so of the baptism, Rolfe was to marry Pocahontas.

Rolfe had arrived in Virginia in 1610. Ambitious and hardworking, he was much respected by the colonists.

Known for his interest in tobacco, Rolfe believed it could be highly profitable for the colonists to grow it. There was a good market for tobacco in England.

Rolfe first met Pocahontas at the church in

Henrico. He also saw her at Rock Hall, the home of the Reverend Whitaker. Rolfe was a religious man. He is likely to have read to Pocahontas from the Bible. He helped her to learn to speak English.

Rolfe was also a lonely man. His wife had died soon after they arrived in Jamestown. Their infant daughter had also died.

After a time, Rolfe found himself falling in love with Pocahontas. But his feelings confused him. He was an English gentleman. As such, he was not supposed to fall in love with a brown-skinned Powhatan. Rolfe didn't know what to do.

Pocahontas, meanwhile, found herself drawn to Rolfe.

Rolfe eventually decided that it was God's will that he marry Pocahontas. He wrote to Sir Thomas Dale asking permission to do so.

Dale was quick to give his approval. Dale saw the marriage as being helpful to the colony. He declared that it would be for the "good of this plantation, for the honour of our countrie [country], and for the glory of God."

Then Rolfe sought out Pocahontas. He was thrilled when she accepted his proposal.

Sir Thomas Dale decided that Pocahontas's father should be told of the upcoming marriage. No one had heard from the Powhatan for many months.

In March 1614, Dale, Pocahontas, and Rolfe boarded the *Treasurer*. Captain Argall was in command. They sailed for Werowocomoco. One hundred and fifty men sailed with them.

The *Treasurer* anchored off Werowocomoco. Dale sent messengers to Powhatan. They told the Supreme Chief that they had brought Pocahontas. In return, they wanted "the promised return of men and arms." Powhatan answered by having his warriors fire arrows at the English.

Dale's response was to attack. He sent his men into the Powhatan settlement. They burned about forty houses. Several Powhatans were wounded or killed.

Then Dale received word that two of Pocahontas's brothers wished to come aboard the *Treasurer*. They were eager to see their sister. They wanted to find out how she "had been used" by the English. Dale called a truce.

Her brothers found Pocahontas in a sour mood. She told them that she was saddened because her father had refused to exchange English guns for her release. She had waited and waited, she said. But she was through waiting. She had been treated well by the English. She was going to remain with them.

Dale sent Rolfe and another colonist ashore to meet with Powhatan. Powhatan refused to see the two men. Since he was Supreme Chief, he would speak only with Dale, the supreme chief of the English.

Rolfe, however, sent a messenger to Powhatan to tell him of his upcoming marriage to Pocahontas. The colonists were back in Jamestown when they heard from Powhatan. The Supreme Chief said he was pleased that Pocahontas planned to marry an Englishmen. He took it as a sign of friendship. He was prepared to end hostilities. He even promised to return some guns.

Powhatan said, however, that he would not

attend the wedding. He had made a solemn promise never to set foot in an English settlement. But Powhatan said he would send one of his brothers in his place.

Pocahontas and John Rolfe were married on April 5, 1614. She was about nineteen.

The wedding took place in the little church in Jamestown. Many settlers attended the ceremony. So did two of Pocahontas's brothers. A sister and her uncle were also on hand.

According to John Smith, writing later of the ceremony, Pocahontas wore a "tunic of Dacca muslin, a flowing veil and long robe of rich material from England."

About her neck, Pocahontas wore a string of freshwater pearls. The glittering pearls were a gift from her father.

The bridegroom slipped the wedding ring upon the bride's finger. "With this ring, I thee wed," he said.

Some time after the wedding, Sir Thomas Dale sent Ralph Hamor to see Powhatan. On Dale's

Pocahontas's marriage to John Rolfe ushered in a long period of generally peaceful relations between the colonists and the Powhatans.

behalf, Hamor asked Powhatan if his youngest daughter might be available for marriage. Powhatan said no. That daughter was already promised in marriage to a chief. Besides, he had already given one daughter to the English. That was enough.

Powhatan asked Hamor for news of Pocahontas.

Hamor replied that Pocahontas was "contented." She had no thought of returning to live among her own people.

According to Hamor, Powhatan laughed at this news. Then the Supreme Chief asked Hamor to take a message back to Dale. "There have bin [been] too many of [your] men and mine slaine [slain], and by my occasion there shall never bee [be] more . . . for I am now olde [old] and would gladly end my daies [days] in peace."

Powhatan's words did not put a complete stop to the fighting between the English and Powhatans. There were still clashes from time to time. But generally the two groups lived together as friends.

The colonists called this period the Peace of Pocahontas. It lasted for as long as she was to live.

A VISIT TO
ENGLAND

AFTER THEIR MARRIAGE, THE ROLFES lived happily. They built a home on the banks of the James River not far from Henrico.

They called their new home "Varina." Varina was the name of a type of tobacco grown by Rolfe.

Growing tobacco kept Rolfe busy. He experimented with different kinds of seeds. He tested a variety of soils. He tried planting at different depths.

Thanks mostly to Rolfe's work, Virginia planters began growing tobacco of high quality. Soon Virginia tobacco was in demand in England. The profits made the colony's planters rich. The tobacco plant came to be known as Virginia's "golden weed."

In 1615, Pocahontas gave birth to a son. The Rolfes named him Thomas.

With the coming of peace in Virginia, leaders of the colony planned further growth. They talked of building a school in Henrico. English and Powhatan children could be taught religion there.

Raising funds for the school was a problem. King James had little interest in the colony. He refused to provide any support.

Sir Thomas Dale and other colonial leaders turned to Pocahontas. Why not take her, her husband, and their son to England? There Pocahontas could be presented to royalty. She could meet the clergy and business leaders. In that way, she could awaken interest in the colony and its needs.

Sir Thomas Dale was planning to return to England. He proposed that the Rolfes go with him. They agreed. In the spring of 1616, the Rolfes sailed for England aboard the *Treasurer*.

About a dozen Powhatan men and women sailed

In 1616, John Rolfe and Pocahontas decided to sail to England. They would bring their one-year-old son, Thomas, with them.

with them. They included Pocahontas's sister Matachanna. She served as baby Thomas's nanny.

Powhatan sent a special representative. His name was Tomocomo. Powhatan wanted Tomocomo to bring back information about England. What was it like? How many people lived there? Powhatan gave Tomocomo a long stick. On it Tomocomo was to make notches to stand for the number of English people he saw.

Powhatan also asked Tomocomo to seek out news about John Smith. Was he dead or alive?

When Pocahontas arrived, she created a sensation. The English had seen Native Americans before. But none were like Lady Rebecca, as Pocahontas was known. She was a princess. On her arrival, she was gowned from head to toe. The English were awed by her regal look.

The Powhatans traveling with Pocahontas wore little. Their bare skin was decorated with splashes of paint. In their hair, they wore clumps of feathers.

Tomocomo drew gasps of amazement. He painted his face and body in bright colors. He gathered his long hair at the back of his neck and tied it with the skin of a weasel and a stuffed snake.

As soon as he arrived, Tomocomo began counting the people he saw. There were so many that he became confused. He tossed away the stick that his chief had given him. He later told Powhatan that the people were as numerous "as the stars in the sky, the sand on the beaches, and the leaves on trees."

Pocahontas and her Powhatan companions gazed in wonder at the sights of London. They were stunned by the city's size and great number of buildings. They saw London Bridge. They visited St. Paul's Cathedral and Westminster Abbey.

Many social events were held in Pocahontas's honor. She met the leading members of English society.

The Bishop of London gave a party for her. One of the party guests later wrote that Pocahontas had "carried herself as a Daughter of a King and was accordingly respected [by many] persons of Honour."

The highlight of Pocahontas's stay was a meeting with Queen Anne, the wife of King James. John Smith arranged the visit. Without telling Pocahontas, Smith wrote to the queen. He told her how Pocahontas had come to the aid of the Jamestown colony. He hailed Pocahontas as "the first Virginian

This portrait from The History of Indian Tribes, *published between 1836 and 1842, shows Pocahontas wearing European clothing.*

that ever spake [spoke] English." He reminded the queen that Pocahontas was the first Virginian to have "a child in marriage of an Englishman."

Queen Anne was impressed. She invited Pocahontas to Whitehall Palace, a royal residence.

After several weeks in London, Pocahontas began to feel ill. She was tired from attending the many social events. And she had breathing problems from London's air. It was damp and filled with thick fireplace smoke from thousands of chimneys.

The Rolfes left London and moved to the town of Brentford, several miles away. Pocahontas found herself surrounded by trees. The air was cleaner. There were open spaces. Pocahontas was happier there.

GRAVESEND

NOT LONG AFTER THE ROLFES settled in Brentford, a visitor called upon them. It was Captain John Smith.

Pocahontas had not seen Captain Smith for eight years. She had no warning of his visit. When he suddenly appeared, she was overcome with emotion. She could not speak. She put her hands to her face and turned away. Then she excused herself and went to her room.

Several hours passed. Only then could she bring herself to speak with him.

Pocahontas began by explaining that the English "did tell us alwaies [always] that you were dead...." She said that the Powhatans did not believe that rumor, however. "Your countriemen [countrymen] will lie much," she said.

She referred to Smith as her "father." That was a term of great respect.

But Smith had not always lived up to her expectations. She reminded him of promises he had made. "You did promise Powhatan what was yours should bee [be] his, and he the like to you. . . ."

Yet Pocahontas pledged that she would "bee [be] forever and ever your countrieman [countryman]."

Not long after, their conversation ended. Smith left Brentford. Pocahontas never saw him again.

In the days that followed, Pocahontas's health continued to decline. Many historians believe she suffered from tuberculosis, a lung disease. Tuberculosis was common in England at the time.

Despite his wife's illness, Rolfe began planning for his family's return to Virginia. He was anxious to continue his life there.

By the second week of March 1617, preparations had been completed. The Rolfes boarded Samuel

Argall's ship the *George* for the Atlantic crossing. By this time, baby Thomas and Pocahontas's sister were also ill.

When the *George* left its London dock, Pocahontas rested in her cabin. She was too sick to even take a last look at the city.

The *George* sailed down the Thames River toward the open sea. The ship approached Gravesend, not far from the mouth of the Thames. By this time, Pocahontas's condition was much worse. She was in desperate need of a doctor.

The *George* dropped anchor off Gravesend. Pocahontas was brought ashore. She was quickly taken to a nearby inn.

A doctor was called. But it was too late. At the age of twenty-one, Pocahontas died.

At the end, she tried to comfort her husband. She told him "all men must die." And she pointed to young Thomas, saying that he was his father's best hope. "'Tis enough that the childe [child] liveth," she said.

Pocahontas was laid to rest in a burial vault of

Pocahontas's son Thomas stands at her side in this portrait, which may have been painted during her visit to the Rolfe family home in 1616.

St. George's church in Gravesend. "Poor little maid," said John Smith. "I sorrowed much for her thus early death . . . for I felt toward her as if she were mine own daughter."

Not long after Pocahontas's funeral, John Rolfe sailed for Virginia aboard the *George*. He had to leave two-year-old Thomas behind. The child was too ill to make the ocean crossing. Thomas was raised in England by Rolfe's brother.

The *George* arrived in Virginia late in May 1617. Rolfe found the Powhatans very friendly. The Peace of Pocahontas continued.

Rolfe sent word to Powhatan telling him of the death of Pocahontas. Powhatan no longer lived at Werowocomoco. He had moved north to a settlement on the banks of the Potomac River.

Moreover, Powhatan had passed his power as Supreme Chief to his brothers, Opitchapan and Opechancanough. Less than a year later, in April 1618, Powhatan died. He was about eighty years old.

Opechancanough had no love for the English. The first English settlers had landed in Jamestown ten years before. From the day of their arrival, Opechancanough had wanted to drive them into the sea. With Powhatan's death, Opechancanough was free to do as he pleased. He began organizing Powhatan warriors for a surprise attack.

By this time, the Virginia colony included about 1,250 men, women, and children. The colony had long since outgrown the original settlement. Large farms called plantations were scattered up and down the James River. They covered an area of more than 100 miles.

On March 22, 1622, the Peace of Pocahontas ended abruptly. Without warning, Opechancanough launched an attack. His goal was to destroy the colony. More than 300 settlers were killed.

Afterward, King James took drastic action. He voided the charter of the Virginia Company. Virginia became a crown colony, controlled by the king.

No longer were the Powhatans to be looked upon as "noble creatures." No longer were the colonists to try to "civilize" them. Now the Powhatans were to be considered no more than fierce savages. The colonists were free to "beat the Salvages [savages] out of the country." As Captain Smith wrote, "... it is more easie [easy] to civilize them by conquest than faire [fair] means."

After the massacre of 1622, the colonists struck back. They attacked and killed many Powhatans. They destroyed their villages and food supplies.

In the years that followed, the settlers kept the Powhatans under constant pressure. The natives were forced to give up the fertile valleys that had been their homeland.

Meanwhile, Jamestown prospered. Tobacco became the leading cash crop.

In 1635, Rolfe's son, Thomas, returned to Virginia. He was twenty years old.

Thomas's grandfather, Powhatan, had left him thousands of acres of land. Like his father, Thomas Rolfe became a planter, growing tobacco.

Thomas Rolfe married Jane Poythress, an Englishwoman. They raised a family. Many hundreds of their descendants live on today.

POCAHONTAS REMEMBERED

AFTER HER DEATH IN 1617, THE legend of Pocahontas began to grow. Generation after generation praised her for her brave rescue of John Smith. She also won fame for her role in helping Jamestown to survive and prosper. Pocahontas came to be looked upon as America's first heroine.

Biographies of her appeared. Novelists gave romance and excitement to her story. Portrait painters added glory and glamour.

Pocahontas's likeness was used to sell cigars and medicines. Towns, cities, and counties adopted her name. During the Civil War, her image appeared on Confederate currency.

A Boston schoolgirl named Mary Woodbury painted this oil portrait of Pocahontas during the 1730s.

Today, everyone knows Pocahontas's name. She will forever be linked to the first English colonies in America. Like Paul Revere and Davy Crockett, she is part of American folklore.

The world of Pocahontas lives on in museums and historic sites. Some of these tell the story of Jamestown, the first permanent English colony in America. Others reveal the culture of the Powhatans.

Tidal currents in the James River have swept away some of the land on which the Jamestown settlement once stood. It was long believed that the original fort had washed into the river. But in 1996, clues that revealed the location of the original fort were discovered.

Archaeologists began digging. In the years since, hundreds of thousands of artifacts have been found. They tell the story of the harsh daily life in Jamestown.

Today, visitors to Jamestown can watch the archaeologists at work. A visitor's center and laboratory display some of their most exciting finds.

In 1957, the state of Virginia celebrated the 350th anniversary of the arrival of the first settlers at Jamestown. The state built what is now known as the Jamestown Settlement. It is about one mile from the original Jamestown site.

Jamestown Settlement is a living history museum.

Archaeologists have erected this string of posts along the James River to show where the southwest wall of the original Jamestown fort once stood.

It offers a re-created Powhatan village. It is like the village in which Pocahontas grew up. There is also a reconstructed English fort on the site.

Replicas of the three ships that brought the first colonists to Jamestown are at the settlement's piers. Going aboard these vessels gives one a taste of shipboard life in the 1600s.

Henrico has not been forgotten. At Henrico, the English built their second major settlement in America.

Henrico was about fifty miles northwest of Jamestown. It was located on a bluff overlooking the James River.

The original Henrico settlement is being reconstructed within the Henricus Historical Park. The park welcomes visitors.

Tribes that were once part of the Powhatan empire now live on Virginia reservations. A treaty that dates to 1646 created the reservations.

The Pamunkey Reservation is northeast of Richmond. It covers 1,100 acres. Visitors are gladly received. The reservation museum presents tools, pottery, and clothing from early times.

The 125-acre Mattaponi Reservation is farther to the east. A museum there displays a necklace of small beads. "Worn by Princess Pocahontas in 1607," says a handwritten note.

These historical sites tell the story of the first Jamestown colonists and the Powhatan people they met. They help us to better understand these two cultures.

CHRONOLOGY

1595
or 1596   Pocahontas is born in what is now Virginia.

1607   Learns that English settlers have arrived to establish a colony at Jamestown.

1608   Saves Captain John Smith from execution.

1608   Brings food to Jamestown to aid struggling colonists.

1609   Warns John Smith that her father has ordered his death.

1610   Is married to Kocoum, who may have been a Patawamake.

1613   Is kidnapped and brought to Jamestown and, later, Henrico.

1614   Is baptized; marries John Rolfe.

1615   Gives birth to a son named Thomas Rolfe.

1616   Travels to London, England, to win support for the Virginia colony.

1617   Dies in Gravesend, England.

1635   Pocahontas's son, Thomas Rolfe, returns to Virginia.

BIBLIOGRAPHY

Primary Sources

Barbour, Philip L., editor. *The Complete Works of Captain John Smith (1580–1631).* Three Volumes. Chapel Hill: University of North Carolina Press, 1986.

Smith, John. *Captain John Smith's Generall Historie of Virginia: A Selection.* Indianapolis: Bobbs-Merrill, 1970.

Note: For a state-by-state (or, in Canada, a province-by-province) listing of libraries, colleges, historical societies, and other institutions where primary sources can be found, visit this Web site: *www.uidaho.edu/special-collections/east2.html*

Secondary Sources

Barbour, Philip L. *Pocahontas and Her World.* Boston: Houghton Mifflin, 1970.

Mossiker, Frances. *Pocahontas: The Life and Legend.* New York: Knopf, 1976.

Rasmussen, William and Robert Tilton. *Pocahontas: Her Life and Legend.* Richmond: Virginia Historical Society, 1994.

Rountree, Helen. *Pocahontas's People: The Powhatan Indians of Virginia Through Four Centuries.* Norman: University of Oklahoma Press, 1990.

Woodward, Grace Steele. *Pocahontas.* Norman: University of Oklahoma Press, 1969.

FURTHER READING

Bulla, Clyde Robert. *Pocahontas and the Strangers*. New York:
    Scholastic Books, 1971.

Fritz, Jean. *The Double Life of Pocahontas*. New York: Puffin
    Books, 1987.

Holler, Anne. *Pocahontas: Powhatan Peacemaker*. Philadelphia:
    Chelsea House, 1993.

Iannone, Catherine. *Pocahontas: The True Story of the Powhatan
    Princess*. Philadelphia: Chelsea Juniors, 1996.

Wilkie, Katherine W. *Pocahontas: Indian Princess*. Champaign,
    Illinois: Garrard Publishing, 1969.

FOR MORE INFORMATION

Jamestown-Yorktown Foundation
Request a brochure titled "Jamestown Settlement"

P. O. Box 1607
Williamsburg, VA 23187
Phone: (888) 593-4682
Web site: http://www.historyisfun.org

Association for the Preservation of Virginia Antiquities
Request brochures titled "Jamestown, America's Hometown" and
"Welcome to Jamestown"

204 West Franklin St.
Richmond, VA 23220-5012
Phone: (804) 648-1889

The Henricus Foundation
Request a brochure titled "The 1611 Citie of Henricus"

P. O. Box 523
Chesterfield, VA 23832
Phone: (804) 706-1340

ACKNOWLEDGMENTS

Many people helped me in providing background information and photographs to be used in this book. Special thanks are due Debby Padgett, Jamestown-Yorktown Foundation; Bryan Green, Virginia Historical Society; Howell Perkins, Virginia Museum of Fine Arts; Audrey Johnson, Library of Virginia; Jennifer Tolpa, Massachusetts Historical Society; Mike Litterst and Diane Stallings, National Park Service, Jamestown; Maja Keech, Library of Congress, Stuart E. Brown, Jr., The Pocahontas Foundation, and Sal Alberti and James Lowe, James Lowe Autographs.

PHOTO CREDITS

Library of Congress: 9, 94; New York Public Library: 13, 31, 37, 41, 44, 65; George Sullivan: 15, 15 (inset), 20, 23, 60, 71, 79, 86, 118; Library of Virginia: 26, 57, 111; Scholastic Inc./Jim McMahon: 34; Virginia Historical Society: 48, 91, 103, 106; Jamestown-Yorktown Foundation: 52, 99; Virginia Museum of Fine Arts: 77; Massachusetts Historical Society: 116.

INDEX

Bold numbers refer to photographs

ABOUT THE AUTHOR

George Sullivan is the author of a good-sized shelf of books for children and young adults. They cover a wide range of topics, from witchcraft to nuclear submarines; from baseball and field hockey to photography.

His interest in photography goes beyond just writing about it. He often takes photos to illustrate his books.

His other titles for Scholastic include *Mr. President: Facts and Fun About the Presidents*, *100 Years in Photographs*, and *Alamo!*

For the In Their Own Words series, he has written biographies of Paul Revere, Lewis and Clark, Abraham Lincoln, Helen Keller and Harriet Tubman.

Mr. Sullivan was born in Lowell, Massachusetts, and brought up in Springfield, where he attended public school.

He graduated from Fordham University and worked in public relations in New York City before turning to writing on a full-time basis.

Mr. Sullivan lives in New York City with his wife. He is a member of PEN, the American Society of Journalists and Authors, and the Authors Guild.